# Stealing Hymnals from the Choir

by

Timothy Martin

*Awarded the 2010 FutureCycle Poetry Book Prize*

**Future**Cycle Press
futurecycle.org

Stealing Hymnals from the Choir

Published by FutureCycle Press
Cave Spring, Georgia, U.S.A.

ISBN: 978-0-9828612-2-6

*For Dorothy, Adam, and Emily*

# Contents

# Shipwreck Survivors March along the Coastline

Three days, twelve days, a lifetime.
To starboard, the sea that didn't bury us.
To port, a land that won't let us pierce it.
Sand beats our shoes with microscopic hammers
until the leather flies in strips. The sun
doesn't search hard enough for clouds to hide it.
We take turns carrying the child on our backs.

For food, cousins of plums that hang on bushes
like the crooked scarecrows of beetles.
Cook samples one and expires on the spot.
Meanwhile, crimson figs stand in trees
whose trunks grow an assortment of cutlery.
The birds that seem to have no song
eat these and stare.

For water, inland springs… only half a day's march.
One of us throws his face down into them,
does not rise. Perhaps he is trying to catch
a gudgeon with his teeth. Perhaps he will;
we leave him to his luck.

At night, we make fires to keep back
the animals that snarl or laugh from the brush,
or both. We throw on buttons, fallen teeth,
the ship's log, sextant, stewpot.
To atone for the lack of wood, the carpenter
throws himself on.

Day sixteen: a sail on the horizon.
We hoist the child to our shoulders, who
tries to do a dance. The sail immediately

slips away, as if it's seen better.
That afternoon, mollusks are exposed
by the tide. When we lunge, they
burrow into the sand like the tongues
of repentant gossips. We strike at the beach,
whose enormous face cannot feel it.

We march. No crossroads, no reckoning, no end.
The child is dead, but we have forgotten
how not to carry him. The captain
walks into the water until he can float his hat.
The second mate dashes himself on the rocks.
Soon it's just the bosun and I. He climbs
invisible rigging to the sky,
reaches a hand for me to follow him.

## The Ex-Lover Speaks

Let me prepare the bed for you, and him.
The pillowcases plucked from the laundry hamper
at the plague ward. The pillows
stuffed with surly woodpeckers.
Sheets that sew themselves to the bed
at the first signs of passion
that would throw them off. At the foot,
in a lean-to of covers, a single scorpion.
This to demonstrate fairest play,
as there's a chance it will miss
twenty toes rolling like dice.
Somewhere in the mattress (your guess),
an alarm that trips 911, brings a hundred
wide-jawed firemen falling through the door.
The whole frame from the wood of trees
where they hung innocent men, their groans escaping
each time you roll over, reach to the lamp.

And in all the spaces beyond you too...
The phone that rings at inextricable moments,
only wrong numbers from madmen.
The curtains flying open whenever
an endearment is uttered. The dog
that keeps dragging dead things to
the door, then barks for you to come striding,
shovel in hand.

## Black Widower

The man who once had a gold ring slipped
from his finger in broadest daylight
takes a Louisville Slugger to the visitor
presumptuously unpacking in the backyard.
There, spinning silk where the line
syringes electricity into the house.
Who'd ever accuse him of cruelty?
His kids play there, and it's allowed
that you reduce things to finest print when
debating real estate with something
that's deadly. No one counts
whether the bat comes down once, twice
more than necessary, and to measure
degrees of upward arc past the point
of efficiency would take a geometrician
bathed in philosophy, and
there's no one like that here. He
crushes the hourglass on her back,
sees to it that her surplus legs
get glued to the June grass.
Afterwards, he wipes blood and venom
from the bat, a job well done, turning
the wood in a shirt that smelled
of lilacs once. He walks to the house
to boil potatoes until they sigh
and give up their skins.

# Trustee

The bride's posy hangs from a basement nail,
upside-down, brown, a clutch of dead tied sparrows.
Lack of romance is not to be inferred; just haste,
to move cross-country, whither we were to have
sent it by delicate, but most urgent, post. Three
anniversaries, and several shades of intensity, ago.

Dear friend, all must be well. It must be
that he does not yet resemble these, rising
from bed in the morning. Nor that his relatives,
staying the weekend, occupy the house
like hippos in a birdbath. Nor that he has
driven a fiery red sports car to the door
as you were counting bills on the kitchen table
to have the bellicose woodchuck removed from the attic.
You do not wish to have this thing,
mournful, redolent of regret,
to diminish the measure of your fresh-cut days.

For your sake, I have forgotten your address.
I have affixed all my stamps to the bottom
of the coffee table. I have slit my packing-boxes
with an assassin's swipe, and moved half-
a-gas-tank's ride from the closest post office.
And so know that all is well here too.
And I will bear this talisman of dismay for you,
because it was my charge, because I am
beyond its effects, because it takes up no space,
because you have not asked for it.

# Two-Timing the Beekeeper

Of all the unwise things you have ever done
(and that counts the time you threw the lit dynamite stick
and forgot your setter loping beside you
or the time you went ice fishing in May
wearing the boots with the heating coils)
this was the most foolish:
to dally with the blue-lipped waitress from *Spud World*
while the other one waited. Nine o'clock, eleven o'clock,
you're not showing. It is this other, recall,
who has your pager number, six pairs of panties
in your dresser, your license plate tattooed
on her forearm, and, most seriously,
a million minions living in her backyard.
She can arrange it so they come down the chimney
buzzing her invective to you, that you lift
a toothbrush full of them in the morning.
That they hide in all your hats and compliment you
on the painted O'Keefe flowers on the wall.
That, in stations of ardor before the fireplace,
the blue-lipped girl gets one caught in her mouth
just before . . . well, dreadful indeed to relate.

Or alternatively (you choose which is worse), she can see
that you never taste honey again.

## The King's Cellars

Working downward... first the throne room
overturned, then the queen hung by association
via her wardrobe dangled from open windows...
the crowd at last arrives. Forty thousand
bottles, some with tenderer cradles than
the infants in the district. The coup leaders
do not wish to deny the people, oh no.
Rather, to save the people from themselves.
They post guards, who get drunk on the job.
More guards, who pass bottles over
their prone comrades to the crowd. The leaders
wall up the rooms. Someone bores holes,
which felicitously decork several bottles.
Mouths volunteer at the holes, curious
to know what vinegar does not taste like.
The leaders dismantle the walls, smash
the bottles as souvenirs of a distasteful time.
The liquid flows to the streets, overstrains
the gutters. Soon the horses refuse to pull
the haywains. More than one citizen dips
his bucket, miles from a useful well.
As quietly as a nurse enters a sickroom,
the leaders settle machine guns on the rooftops.

# Ghost Town Fire

It starts in the blacksmith's shop, the furnace
that the old man (he and his wife
volley a few words daily to keep voices limber
for the rare tourist) left going at lunch.
The week's one newsworthy breeze
carries the sparks to the floor, where
a few crooked planks shovel them on to the rest.

Fire unzips the building that hands
had struggled hard to fasten years before.
Down the line it goes, the bank, livery,
dry saloon... the flames in yellow-and-ochre
beachballs that deflate the catchers.
The telegraph office, off life support
long since, goes. Smoke spills
its inkpot into the empty sky,
and no one around to construe it.

The whole town's halved, then halved
again. The nearest firehouse
forty miles to the east and not enough water
in the town to save the broom closet,
the broom. The church is converted
last of all, mounting to the sky
a reluctant beat behind the rest. Only
the tombstones behind it endure.
By dusk, ashes will have started over
in the next valley as apprentice sand.
It's how a thing should end:
in full light, a dash to the finish,
those who once inhabited
outnumbering those who mourn.

# The Death of Aeschylus

An ending entirely too fictional
for one of his own plays. He was walking
the shore, doubtlessly drumming on the tragic,
when the green bolt struck from the sky.
His bald head was all bull's-eye, no target,
and it failed to yield to the one turtle with wings
in the Aegean's otherwise no-nonsense blue.
Like all jokes it needed perfect timing,
which the eagle provided with a graceful exit-glide.
Don't ask about the funeral: the mourners
biting their lips, relatives whistling
and looking away, tears (not of grief)
threatening the flames on the pyre.

Yet allow him the last word.
He might insist that a hollow laugh is
a brick that's short the building, how the thing
mustn't light without bending the branch.
So say instead that this is how inspiration goes.
You're at the watery impasse, muddled
for a moment, when something on high
chooses to let the notion fly. You stagger crosswise,
stunned, and a good thing, for then you miss
how the greater part of the meat is falling away
unused. Meanwhile the gods, still hungry,
have flown to the next valley. And you're left to
lonely eurekas for the piece of itself
that heaven let fall, then forgot.

# The Man Who Fell Asleep Inside a Moose

Because he was cold, that's why.
This being Alaska, and several decades
before it would dawn on Holiday Inn that
hypothermic tourists too needed a place to stay.
He improvised, leagues from the nearest anywhere,
by slicing the bull lengthwise and crawling in
to crib fleeting warmth from the voided carcass.
So it wasn't any primal stab at consorting
with antlered spirits. He was cold, that's why.
For shamanism read shortsightedness,
or if you're in a mood to be charitable,
greenhorn ingenuity that soured.
Because in the morning he found it had frozen
around him, thus impeding efforts to escape.
Then a bad day turned worse.
First one snout appeared outside, then another,
then another. And so he passed
into the mythology of the wolves after all.
For generations on spoke they spoke in awe
of the marvelous beast that gave birth once
to an oddity not its own, but which was found
to be at hand, wriggling, and wholly satisfactory.

# Eighth Rest

The assassin hesitates, looking at the gun
in his hand. He expected to find a pencil there,
to write more of the sugary sonnets he'd given
his landlady after she'd mended his overcoat
for no good reason. Or an eggbeater,
to make his nephews tapioca to eat
on the terrace while they watched the peacocks.
Which reminds him he's intended
to send his sister his second wheelbarrow,
hers being rusted through like a cancerous jaw.
His boot is temporarily caught between
the floorboards of time; if he's to step ahead,
it'll have to be awkwardly, with one
stockinged foot. The breeze has stilled.
Two more notes, and the parade
will have passed. The widow is already
behind schedule for her weeping.

# Pet Store Expecting Fish Gets Man's Body

An honest mistake, a back turned at the warehouse
(and a thousand apologies from the shipper).
Not, we assure you, the work
of tragicomic gangsters, who did not fully grasp
the principle of sending one to sleep with...
well, in no wise was it. We are mortified
at the thought of the college student,
crowbar still in her fist, passed out next to
the crate in your back room. We deeply regret
the youngsters leaving empty-handed,
pulled puddle-eyed past cages of dogs
with snouts like black armbands against the wire.
We cannot, however, at present rectify it.
In Keokuk, they expected Uncle Chester, and were
surprised to unpack instead coral, koi
waving *konichiwa*, seahorses like darning needles
quickening the water. They've set
the aquarium in the funeral parlor,
where the bier was to be. The family
dances in slow undulations, the gulls
of grief kept circling high above.

# The Untruth

First one, then another of us, said it.
Words we assumed were to soothe…
talk of therapy and melioration, the too-bright
tablecloth you spread sometimes when mortality
throws an awkward come-as-you-are party.

She watched from under hospital white,
eyes extra-quick, as if the body had
donated to them the surplus movement
it wouldn't get around to using now. They were
sharpshooters, double agents that swiftly
exposed the bullshit we were saying,
as nurses and IV's threaded each other around the bed.

We made a pact of the untruth.
It was the bread we baked
because *we* were hungry. A bedtime story
to send the teller to sleep, getaway car
speeding from the vault still brimming with gold.
We could have at least chosen silence,
chose to help each other rise and walk instead.

# You Had to Ask

You ask for a booth in the restaurant,
and they hand you a pair of stilts and a plate
to wobble on the end of your nose.
You order a pair of rollerblades, and they
deliver a kayak that takes off your doorframe
as they carry it in. You tell the shop
to change your motor oil, they rip up
the upholstery and put in howdahs
front and back with prickly, straw-sewn seats.
You ask your optometrist about your vision,
he prescribes glasses chipped
from mica gathered on an outcrop
of Mt. Etna. And a nose job.

You go looking for love—bottles of Bordeaux shared,
toes locking beneath a lazy Sunday sheet.
You find envelopes of sulfuric acid
mailed to your nubby fingertips, something
that alternates between an anvil and a shooting star
that you carry in the empty jar of your chest.

# Hero Worship

They're a people we can justly admire.
Their ancient gods were wiser than ours, had
brighter teeth, clutched more clement laws
to their granite chests. Their scientists were parsing
the genes of damselflies at the same time
that ours were proving the sun was not a pinwheel.
Their navigators had instituted the saffron trade
when ours were still working out
why their stone boats sank in the harbor.
We were vexed in our attempts to raise cabbages;
they invented iron smelting, hair dryers, mutual funds.
They heaped ziggurats up to the ozone;
we built shelters for our widows only if first
the tree fell. Their virgins were more virginal,
their playwrights droller, their senators more articulate.
For all this and more we admire them,
who welcome now our planes laden
with bananas and blue jeans, and use
our language to send their infants to sleep.

# Cape of Another's Hopes

From the boat's deck, no less verdant
than they'd promised at home,
that place that had discharged us
with a thousand well-wishes
(half a wish per soul). Once ashore,
a week clearing grass sharper than our blades,
a month felling trees (the monkeys sulking
to higher ground), and we'd approximated
the village they had drawn on the meeting
room wall, when they'd set down teacups
to argue over T-square and pen.

Then came the rain. Rain like hawks' beaks, rain
like stones. Sleep not coming, as lightning sketched
bright stick figures against the closed eyelid.
Our rice, washed away in midget flotillas
to the lagoon. The day's work became
preserving the axes and hoes from rusting.
From home they sent a ship
laden with hospital gauze and sheet music.

When the sun's stubborn candle emerged,
we moved to cooler ground. As if fending
off loneliness, so did the mambas, kraits,
and a hundred (it must make a difference to them)
types of ants. A particular small spitting cobra,
the color of the hair ribbons we kept,
made unfortunate confusion for the young girls
who reached too quick a hand. A thousand
miles away, there was a subscription ball
to send us cheesecloth and Christmas trees.

Taking up the ground we'd otherwise give to planting:
the sexton, flax dresser, nurseryman, tailor.
The piano tuner, the stockbroker. The baker's
middle daughter, carefully plucked from the batch.
When the dancing master (whom
they would not let us board without) goes,
the macaws in the trees will be silent for an hour.

## The Accompanist

lassos her piano and makes it wait
for these soloists: scared-shitless kids
who'd rather mom and dad right now
were stalled on an arctic icebreaker,
or orbiting the far side of Triton,
instead of beaming in the audience
like a couple of mortifying searchlights.
She downshifts Hindemith to pick up the boy
who's hitchhiking through the piece and got
stranded about four bars back. She slips blinders
on a galloping rondo and persuades it
to pull another, who's loaded a heap of notes
into the wagon and hopped on.
When "Traumerei" bespeaks life just above absolute zero,
instead of in dreams, she's hardly perturbed.

She's a marvel of adaptation, and all need her.
These, to steady the net so they can land
in one piece on the other side
of Saint-Saens. The hearers, to keep disaster
at finger's length, barely, blessedly out of reach.

All the while, she has to still her own soul,
detour her passion to another place and time.
Because the sixteenth notes are ready to riot,
overpower their prison guard so
they can drink down blue sky. And oh!
those arpeggios! they ought to be
worn like pearls
against a sonata's sleek dress.
But not now. She has her job,

which is to rescue beauty where it lies.
A promise will have to do:
*meet me later in the boathouse, Ludwig,*
*when the children are all asleep.*

# Inventory

From my elderly father's shed: an ancient gas mower
with parts Henry Ford might have rejected.
A ladder that groans at you if you unfold it.
A spray can of WD-40 that will need WD-40
to work. Something that is either twine
or talcum powder. A hoe, two leaf rakes,
a shovel that itself will be dug up one day.
Cans of paint that all struggle towards
the same filing-cabinet gray. Screwdrivers
once actually held by Phillips. A weed whacker
it would not trouble your conscience
to give to a child to play with.
Certain lengths of garden hose married
outside their species to other hose.

Like its owner: free of too many splintered surfaces,
locked but lightly, accommodating withal
the shadows lengthening like tarpaper on the walls.

# For Those Who Love

For those who love from the next room, from three
horizons over, who bounce papier-mâché arrows of
affection off the moon's surface, we praise you.

To ones who send flowers by dog-sled around the poles,
who vacillate, who write flirtatious notes
wholly in the subjunctive, we pray for your peace.

For those who tarry, stammer, sleep alone,
whose kisses are best described by trigonometric functions,
who fall on the live grenade of the heart,
we wish you honest breezes and a boat to somewhere.

## Salvage Alongside the Enemy

Raising the fuselage with air bags, sawing off
the wings, winching the engines out with machines
brought swampside...whatever it takes to
lift it from this malarial sump.
The crocodiles prefer to pull
in the counter direction. Scorpions
dead-end themselves in our boots left
standing at the edge. One fewer in
the mess tent, after someone
rummaging for the plane's joystick
plucked out an adder instead.

It takes ten, then twenty, to rock it free,
tumble it onto trucks for a warehouse
where the little boy in someone can't wait
to piece it back whole. Destined
for a museum, to stand polished and quaint,
far removed from here: an eyesore on good days,
a wet suitcase full of ghosts on bad,
two generations after my grandfathers
tried to bomb yours
for a reason that is shut
in the swift cargo holds of the past.

# Geneticists in the Siege

*Leningrad, 1943*

Not one of them, no not one,
was tempted: While the Germans used
church spires to play mumblety-peg,
simplified sandstone walls
to just sand. Backed into
the laboratory, sleepless,
eating at first the chemicals that were safe,
then those that would not kill,
then nothing. While in the vault
hundreds upon thousands of what
they'd sworn to preserve. Seeds
of every edible sort, including those
that (they reasoned) might not occur
elsewhere tomorrow: tomatoes
with the delicate flavor of rain,
a fig pollinated by a certain wasp
whose last member wandered too close
to the shoelace factory's smokestack.
They were not tempted behind
blackened windows, and even bent
their dreams to not be of turnips
roasting or berries with messages waiting
to be decoded by the tongue.

# Hands

When the old woman buries the daughter who
didn't wait her turn for eternity, the brother
(her son) has a problem. How to free hands
rusted with grief to the church pew
when the service is through? He'll try tools
that have never worked between them before:
persuasion, argument, the lever
of one will against the eccentric boulder
of another. She wants to hold on
past the last *amen,* through when the organ
starts to skywrite in satin in the half-filled church.
It'll take a wrench, from deep in a resolute bag
he forgot he had, to yank her away
and turn her to the living. And he's
right too, since the others are waiting to file out
and things need now to lean toward emptiness.

But still, sir, forbear a little. Her hands
will catch up soon enough with the last,
lonely parts of her. In their lifting,
these are one, two, three...
ten flowers that shouldn't have to bloom again.

# The Church of His Debit-Card Soul

In the church of his debit-card soul
(to which he faithfully returns every Sunday),
he listens to the earnest preacher preach
dissertations on sin and its twin, salvation,
and it all feels a little stiff to him, like a knee
that took a bullet aimed at someone else once,
and… wait a minute… repositioning… there, better.
Meanwhile of (to his left) his wife, he wonders
if she notices how the new choir director
looks like he should be on a Greek island
working on his tan's tan and frantically
counts the altos to see if she'd be so inspired.
Of (to his right) his son, he thinks that someday
son will ask for the car keys, and dad will say no,
and the fiasco will end years later in the rest home,
where sonny will switch malarial bilge into his IV
and grease his wheelchair's wheels while looking for
the building's most freshly polished floor.
He doesn't grasp how each of them
would give anything to dare one clear beatitude
of love, or roll away the stone of the heart
and share with him the remarkable,
small "r" resurrection. Later, he'll rise
for an old tuneful hymn and dream of a backyard chair,
of dozing to the hum of another's mower.
Faith, so difficult to unlearn.
So difficult to learn, faith.

# Clams

Eighty-six of his ninety years spent stooping and plucking
clams from the flats at low tide, and not complaining, no,
delighted rather how still once a day heaven
pulled back its coverlet and let mortals
help themselves to what it used an ocean to hide.
Until one time, waders up over stiff joints, beach
to himself, he found in the shallows the once-in-
not-quite-a-century bounty. Quahogs underfoot
thick as cobblestones, enchanted, leaping into his hands
where he stood. He bent over his task like a surgeon,
or Michelangelo seeing David in the marble block
for the first time. And so missed the water returning,
rising around him. Struck for shore, not making it,
but bucket held high between his teeth,
because someone ought to enjoy these splendors,
which later that evening, in a cottage hung with needlework,
steamed and with a good sauterne,
someone surely did.

# Vignette: New Orleans, 1830s

The logic as graceful, as circular, as a dress
turning at a cotillion. And demanded likewise
that gentlemen not stare too closely.
The immigrants digging the canal—slaves
from the outset deemed too dear to spend—
were being felled by yellow fever:
8,000 (to the most traceable digit) dead.
How to assign cause, with pens waiting over ledgers
financial, scientific, moral? The workers
themselves must be to blame, who
with each shovelful pried up gasses
that carried the disease. The logic
as hard as the bread at their tables.
The consequences certain: to the widows,
baskets of salt and molasses; to those left
digging, a dollar a week less,
owing to the business lost to these delays.

# Far North Burial

Not just the landscape sending at times
the wrong signal—*no sunset!*—there are other problems
with getting the dead where they belong.
Such as, the granite that passes itself off as ground
ten frozen months of the year,
successfully folding shovels back
into the diggers' hands. Which is why
the town debates every spring the number
to make, and now, while earth is still open
to the idea. The holes then line the graveyard
like empty slot machine rows waiting for the fruit.

The committee means no ill, it's just good management,
as they name names. Nana Alice,
whose daughter grudgingly gives her
the back bedroom… yes, surely this season.
Ed Deerfoot, who no longer has two teeth
close enough to cast shadows on each other?
Perhaps. If the wind is bitter enough,
his heart may abandon rattling its tin cup
against the bars of his being.

There is one waiting for you, grandfather,
as you turn from snowdrifts
with the uneasy feel of mortuary sheets.
Do not think us loveless if we omit your weight
in planning the trip across the frozen lake.
Or if the caribou haunch is passed
across your lap, to the one with his arm
around a fiancée and eyes like two North Stars
by which we reckon tomorrow.

# Caravaggio Trudged

Up the coast, away from Rome
(the closer destination) and a pardon
(the pope waiting with papers) for his latest crime.
Through the natural corrosives
of sand and salt marsh that the painter in him
must have flinched from.
July, of course—the flies coaxing
an intriguing carmine from his arms—
since the scene must be arranged
for maximum drama.
In pursuit of two canvases, rolled,
which the ship he'd ridden
had continued to clutch after setting him ashore.
One a *St. John* (lost), the other not recorded.
At night, the fever descending, he dreamed
an eagle rent his breast.
Bandits were a threat, though none bothered him,
though if they had, he might have argued
he'd already lost all.
And so died in a hueless hospital bed,
having at least reached the same town
as his paintings. Though he never again
touched them, or gazed on their colors,
or called them to his side saying,
*Let us make peace, now that you will walk*
*the wide world in my place,*
*lacking half of all I meant to give you.*

# Will

A lifetime of acrimony
lasered into a narrow line, ten words,
ten knuckles on the page: *To my son George
the sum of one (1) dollar.* He worked years
on this, setting and resetting the words like
a man moving an acre of bricks six inches left,
then right again. Three years alone
on the opening spondee pair, until
they hung with the precise top-heavy weight
he needed. An entire summer (through lemonade,
crummy novels, mosquito-swatting) debating
zero vs. one, settling on mock munificence
over absence, just as a naked body is more naked
for the bits of cloth that claw about the loins.
Besides, the joke of the parentheses—
plausibly lawyerlike, yet cruel—too good to resist.
This sustained him, nurtured him, through
divorces (*you quarreled with me over
the family business*), cancer (*coveted
my money like a jackal that paradoxically owes its teeth
to the wildebeest it tracks*), forced retirement
(*married a woman who would sooner sacrifice an eye
than receive me civilly at your table*). While
the poison dart, the tiny chicken bone
for a coming throat, waited somewhere
in a bank vault that he checked thrice daily in his mind.

Which his son spoiled by dying first,
word passing through several mouths
to reach him as he ate a grapefruit on the patio.

And he, too late, realizing what accrued,
all which would be spared from separate accounts
of surprise, regret, and yes, of grief.

# Feral

Before the comfort of county lines, the congenial
pillow-fights of property easements, the concept
of suburbs, settlers in proto-Virginia
surrendered livestock to the thickened woods to run.
Not from sloth or failure of imagination, but
for the commonsense reason that land,
that sprawling peasant apron that hides gold in its pockets,
could not be spared to grow their feed.

Cows returned home seldom, pigs less,
exchanging blank stares instead
with the deer and beaver they met in clearings.
Fences erected by neighbors to keep
the unwild *out*, the barnyard as big as
the new land that vanished into shadowy hallways
of the distant mountains.

And the sight of the gentleman, trousers
measled with mud, ankle turned where he tripped
over a hawthorn root. Saddle in hand
as he whistled for Brownie or Danny Boy.
A ride's required to church, before sins sink
like a bucket of carrion knocked into the open well.
Or, today, there are races on the village green.
Two minutes, two swift and dreamlike minutes
of rider and beast, are what's needed
to mend the assumption of dominion.

## Gold Rush Port

Where a hundred, a thousand, land daily,
stay a week, then run upward like
bewitched rain into the hills beyond.
The city strains to keep up.
Mud gets an in-name-only promotion
to street; building timbers are raised while
workers still cling to them, frantically painting.
Barroom, brothel, bank stand on the corner
across from . . . brothel, bank, barroom.
Meanwhile, no one notices how those who
have left are not returning. The schoolmaster
from Texas, twenty leagues off now
with a pickaxe in his back. The dry-goods clerk,
middle-aged and lame, who at this moment
swings his walking-stick at the circle of wolves.
The ships they'd arrived in (we won't need to pass
this way again!) left in the harbor to rot.
Until the enterprising drag them into avenues
to serve as barbershops, restaurants with
outsized chandeliers and beef brought from the East.
A silver dollar buys a table in the crow's nest,
where you can watch evening slip
a pickpocket hand down half-conscious streets.

# Kiss: An Epilogue

After this, there'll be no more, and both
should know it. She receives his kiss
with return-to-sender ardor, he embraces
her as if he'd arms of plywood, breakable.
His mouth's an obstacle course
where there was once ski run; her tongue's
a bird tied by tailfeathers to the nest.
Someone forgot to pay the electric bill.
Each wears the other like an overcoat
found in the bazaar near the sulfur works.
Gunboats guard the coastlines of caresses.
The curtain has come down, the scenery already changed
by unsentimental stagehands of the soul.
She is weary; he thinks of unopened mail at home.
It's all lasted one kiss too long,
the fire leaping backwards to the unstruck match.

# And We Blame You for Our Bad Dancing Too

Thirty-nine of our sheep died,
but only after your carts teetered through
our village like bears with fused toes. Our wheat
was stung with ergot, which must have been caused
by your spittle in the wind from fifty leagues off.
Our milch cows gave only gnat-riddled dust,
because you sang under your breath while braiding rope.
You were spotted near our wells,
after which our dogs turned on us,
preferring our legs to partridge bones.
When snow fell in June, the bride lost her desire,
spiders raced across our thumbs while we turned
pages of Gospel, it was you and your strange concertina music.

Wherefore we have chased you with firebrands
and scythes, and caught straggling bands of you,
and restored our ransomed sun to the heavens above.
Pray God you do not vanish from this earth,
who give our saddlemakers a reason to tend their vats,
our children a reason to love us.

## Exchange

The ones that were lowered into salt mines
by ingenious device of winch, sling, and rope—
the horses and burros who'd stood unluckily in
nearby farms—never again touched surface,
begetting foal and hinny that never, ever
touched surface, pulling by gaslight down there
the wagons and tumbrels that must have been
writ large in dreams. Scratching their backs
on jagged mineral columns (plentiful, ubiquitous),
and eating what could be readily mashed, which
is to say what could be coaxed from provisions
that were threaded down the shaft after them.
While a cruel lot, not an insufferable one
(the salinized air held by some to be fortified,
therapeutic). Until they expired
in the most inapt of settings,
surrounded by a thousand kilotons of cool preservative.

To the childlike, the disingenuous, the mercenary,
it must have seemed a miracle: dispatch
the whinnying, braying form below, and
you pull back an armful of prize. Suitable
for improving tastes, preserving fish, gaining footing,
for double-penalizing your enemy's wounds.

# First Causes

*This reminded her of a preacher who had proved
the existence of God by noting that someone had
placed the rivers near large cities.*
                    —Jennifer Michael Hecht

Let us praise the stomach for being well positioned
to receive the food; the civet for holding still
for her stripes. Let us remark how the tiny catcher's mitt
of a forest lake circles just so underneath the rain.

And publish the story of tides, how they tug at the moon
like fleas hauling a skyscraper. And hang plaques
to the music that circles the earth three times
before seeking out the piano's strings.

Let us marvel at how the shade knows to look
for where the summer moss is growing; how the fleeing train
of the universe slows even for us, who sit
facing backwards, reading yesterday's newspaper.

# The Cartographer's Spleen

With a single stroke, the town of Poetry Tulip
is erased. Likewise Dewy Rose, Hemp, Po Biddy Crossroads.
In Experiment, where the volunteer fire department
occupies the lone burnable building, they cannot withstand.
The space is too dear, the names are starting to cross
and cancel one another. And so these small, jagged ones
must go, like inebriated third cousins you plan
the family reunion one step ahead of, to be fetched
within the borders of East Whatever, Business-as-Usual Falls.
In Cloudland tonight, they will light their lone candle
with the match they've been hoarding behind the tea kettle.
At the farewell party in Sharp Top, someone will
play the fiddle, then hurry to dance with the other
before the notes hitch a ride inside the ceiling, walls.

# Four-Way Stop

which somehow, unfathomably, in an angels-bending-to-tie-
their-shoes moment, she missed. And was spared the memory
of aught else until she awoke, supine, her bones
in archipelagos, having missed her mother's burial
(passenger seat) by two days. And, as if guilt
were moving through the cosmos as easily as
lava through a spun-sugar valley, then
had to endure the days of father with his lover,
for whom she had dusted a place with a noxious cloth
of chance (father becoming suddenly generous at Christmastime,
though meeting all her gazes with eyes hinged on trapdoors).

Chauffeur of causality, crumpled soul, sister to us all,
stop awhile. I would willingly ride with you,
nor ever fault your judgment, nor be amazed at
the acceleration from the intersection of lively things.

# Jellyfish in the Vineyard

*France, c. 1860*

Phylloxera—tiny, wingless—invaded the stock,
held revival meetings on the roots,
where they sucked and sucked until the fruit
deflated, just like the hot-air balloons
that wouldn't be wafting in celebration over Paris,
not this year. So dire was this that
they proposed and/or tried a menu
of non-sequitur remedies. Including moles, ants,
chickens, jellyfish, nicotine, turpentine,
lard, Venus fly-traps, exorcism, mesmerism,
marching bands, volcanic ash (specifically
from Pompeii), schoolboys hired to urinate
on the vines (two sous a delivery), and wheelbarrows
with mallets to beat the ground and drive
the infesters to sea. They clutched at straws,
excluding, inexplicably, straw itself. None
of this released the insects' hold on
the plants. Vats stood vacant, presses dry,
labelless bottles milling aimlessly in storerooms.

It was not the economic loss that offended,
nor again the nails raked across the nose
of cultural and national pride. It was how
the circle, ancient and complicit, had been disturbed.
Without the root, no grape. Without the grape,
no wine. Without the wine, no forgetting one's
troubles at day's end after camembert and crusts
by the fire. Including thoughts of creatures
that wriggle and turn half the land to rust,
and the choice half, at that.

## Nearly Fully Drowned Town

For years the steeple a holy periscope
above the blue, in the valley they purposely
flooded to make a reservoir for other thirsts.
Now the wind, the sun, the irony-loving earth
uncover this place again, too late
for those who left once with laden pushcarts
while dust was yet loitering in their yards.
The water lowered like a queer theater curtain
to many wonders: a trout wriggling
on a fence stake, the lost oar aslant
the roof of the tobacco-curing shed.
Over here, in the deputy mayor's house,
algae on an abandoned dinner plate
as if it's spinach disdained by a sullen child.
The gardens, besotted, may swear off
the stuff forever. A crayfish on a weathervane
is waving a desperate, hitchhiking thumb.
The birds are leagues away now,
croaking how they'll not be fooled again
into nesting in the eaves of the lofty merchant.

## Blessed Be This House Now

which you so generously give us. Where you
toiled and slept, threw parties, served
a hundred score (or more) hypersalted dinners,
made children, raised same, billeted dogs and cats,
lied, loved, rued, and wept. Where the den (what
were you thinking?) is the color of a room
where you practiced detonating pumpkins.
Where you planted a pear tree that lacks tribal memory
of bearing fruit, grew agoraphobic grass, and withal
brought more beauty to this street corner
than it had ever known before you.
Where you paid bills, drank, healed sick, drank more,
hung crooked smiles of Christmas lights.
Where finally you could not keep despair
from entering as if on the sole of a boot
and bending your family down.

We who receive this space will keep it.
We will tighten shingles on the roof
while music is heard from below.
We will throw open shades, evict things that crawl
from the corners, hang paper that refracts
the light fivefold. We will bow low
to spirits that pass us in the hallway, who
claim ownership of the crossed fingers of the wiring,
the basement door shrugged from its frame,
no less than we.

# Visages

Cesare Borgia, right after (a few paltry
days after) he ordered two of his enemies
garotted, and right before (these events
crowding together in his life) he had
nine old women roasted alive
for failing to reveal the location of their money,
received a box from a supporter.
In it: one hundred carnival masks,
with the note that Cesare should take care
not to neglect his entertainment, when
his labors allowed. And he (awareness
of self-irony being the first casualty of war)
handled each of them, marveling how
they resembled this friend or that,
or a shopkeeper in Urbino who had met
his fate unflinchingly once, as Cesare's sword
feigned blushing in the public square.

# Instructions for Crossing the Styx

Arms and legs—or the effluvial aftermath—
inside the boat. You must dispose of refuse,
if you are still clutching the last document
(the contract or now-pointless note to a secret lover)
that you held in life. Not an extraneous shred,
not a notch on a dust mote on a bead of dried ink,
must pass the gates unbidden.

To your left, on the approaching shore,
you see the orchard of suicides. From every branch,
a Judas, a Cato, a Hart Crane. Your guide cannot help
identify them; his mouth was sewn shut with a railroad spike
for speaking ill of the selfless on earth.

For others of you (e.g., those who have been parted
from your eyes), there are smells and sounds
such as the detonation of unachieved dreams
performed by a team of spirits in the distance.
Please do not crowd the soul in front of you;
it may be she who in life made insincere attachments
and will perpetually find her arms two inches too short
to touch another in this place.

In an emergency, do not move
from your place. You cannot again lose
the life already surrendered, though you will find
we have pointedly failed to remove the fear
of such. If the boat founders,
it will crawl the river's bottom,
intent on serving you up on the other side.

Worst is when the pilot, stiff in arm and mind
from the day's crossings, calls for a song.
Then your voice is forced upward like an anvil
through a drinking straw. The notes circle the boat
before turning to a thousand wasps confused
and angry at being so suddenly born.

## Post-Conjugal Sight

Out the window, a single spider's strand
in the branches, presently lacking the rest
of the web. The spider might have lost
its backing mid-project and/or permanently become
somebody else's lunch break.
Or I am looking at old news, the foundation
of a habitable house from which the resident
has long fled. Like this moment between you and me,
there's no convenient wisdom.
Believe the science that tells you how
this string of a ghost-mandolin is the strongest
of substances. Or open the window—
and pass me that shoe fallen on the floor—
and I will show you the contrary.

# Swimming the River with a Spider Monkey on Her Head

She would save it from misuse
in the tiny circus that shuffled
from town to town and pitched its tents
like indiscreet drying laundry.
Where she herself, sequined and barely clad,
appeared nightly in the big cats' cage,
murmuring privileged gossip with them
while the audience clapped. She preferred
impenetrable forests to sleeping,
breathing barely to the other,
and would one day dissolve
more or less for good into a jungle
to see, touch, and live with what dwelled there.
But first this deed, this crawl
over swift water with eyes
shining in the moonlight. For which
the monkey (she would not want it otherwise)
showed gratitude by trying to shred
the planks of its circumscribed ark.

# Project

Not with the one-note arias of saws,
the clumsy flamenco of my hammers,
the secret handshakes of screws
into joists. Nor the artless hanging of
drywall, the clean sweep of the varnish.
Not in the depth, breadth, solidity
of struck space. But rather in
intent, which has no corners;
in the refusal of the tools of duplicity,
the bearing of circumstance continually
exposed to the elements; in the creation
of a place where, when the wind turns in the keyhole,
it does not terrify you to be.

## Potatoes and Guns

The one the gift of a young monk, who simply
wanted to feed them after they'd met his boat
with sunken cheeks, cadaverous, the chief staggering
under the weight of his headdress's feathers.
The other, a fair swap with bearded men
who landed and started asking casual questions
about pearls lying so numerous they got caught
in sandals and irritated their (the natives') toes.

With the two, potatoes and guns, they walked
across the landscape as if in a pair
of oddly matched, though serviceable, boots.
No more starving armies nor needing to walk
backwards to the village after two days,
when the animals learned to hide. The chefs
were second now only to the generals, serving
boiled and baked in the field, along with mashed,
scalloped, hash browns, latke, pommes fondant.
Within six weeks they'd reached the western coast
and taken revenge on the village that had once
stolen their third-best butter churn while they slept.

Thank you, good friar, for your bounty:
brown, versatile, and delicious, like jewels that swell
so easily beneath the earth. You will not be held
accountable in the final reckoning of the bill,
who did not foresee the uses of the human heart
nor how the innocent ox is joined to
the yoke of mischief inside your brother's barn.

## Repeat, No Coda

We who love you have watched you
step on the same garden rake (a hundred times),
slip on the same patch of ice (do you not
own a shovel?), draw your thirty-third traffic ticket
for blundering onto the one-way street,
lose the last copy of the house key you made
from a friend's copy, and once more,
give your heart away as if it were
a kind of dreadful white elephant.

We who love you will go to long lunches with you,
read your e-mails, refuse to check caller ID
before answering the phone. We will listen,
share your sorrow like a bone that's been gnawed
to the thickness of twelve eyelashes,
and not say what we are thinking. Which is,
*Tell him your uncle deeded you a villa*
*on Tierra del Fuego! Creep into your apartment hallway*
*at midnight and exchange door numbers!*
We reason that only under a bewitched moon
does the map contrive to read itself,
the well to draw its own water.
So we persist. These are roads
we could drive with you while blindfolded
or steering with our noses.

We who love you will likewise lose sleep,
easing your night like sentries who
telepathically know when to relieve. We
do this because our own dreams tonight

come in armfuls of broken bottles, because
our neighbor is hosting a party for kettledrum lovers,
because we love you,
because we know that we too are the same.

# Mummers

See how the soul trundles its cart from
place to place, fabricating a stage
from the trees and rocks around it.
A business meeting, lunch with an ex-
(or by the time of coffees and the check, again-future)
lover, talk about ravenous taxes shared
with a neighbor over a moldering leaf pile.
The soul acts its part,
shrugs out of the scratchy bear costume,
and moves on, trailed by silence, applause,
unexpectedly edible cabbages, dogs
whose teeth the bailiff must spend nights sharpening.
The soul takes it in stride, and will
sometimes forget—like any good actor—
where the proscenium stops and the jonquils begin,
convinced that this natural fiction is
its one indelible life.

Then come the evening, a scene that no one sees:
the father in his chair stacking bills and coins
against the day's dusty losses; the little girl
lying on the floor eating an apple and
studying her lines; and mama, mending
a tattered smock (keep your right side
to the audience!), feeling older than
the willow that's keening in the yard,
her eyes starting to go . . .

# From a Description of Itzhak Perlman

*"He plays as if the violin were an extension
of his arms and hands"*

How lovely . . . a glissando when flinging food to the birds,
the dark staccatos of Brahms' concerto
when sawing wood. A single clear note
(C major, pastoral) with each pepper plant seed
dropped into the mucky garden. If
you are a close friend (and only if)
you may pizzicato back when shaking hands.

A wondrous life it would be, tossing off
trills and runs even while scrubbing the cellar stairs.
Although they may not love the little fripperies
(Kreisler a good bet) that cannot be hushed
when the casket is raised in the dolorous church.
No matter that.
Enough that there would be music
from the first lifting of the covers at dawn.
Take my hand, and let the rondos rise
between us as we're walking all paths,
all weather, all moods.

## Portrait of the Artist from One Extant Work

Not a relative of mine but my wife's, who
over a hundred years ago took charcoal
and drew a cat glaring from a candy dish
so lifelike, so true, that the half
to our home who do not take it for a photograph
are reaching frantically for the dinner napkin
to stifle a sneeze.

The family story holding that his wife
sang a smoldering don't-even-think-it torch song,
played a you-have-mouths-to-feed fugue,
to dissuade him from mistaking this pastime
for a career. The drawing's surface like butcher paper;
he may have been were he not
a trolley conductor, were he not a shipping clerk
(the story dropping an incidental stitch
at this point).

Let us see him therefore in a puddle of
weak *fin de siècle* electric light,
the cold knuckles of the radiator behind him,
a baby (we can make it two) crying
in the next room as he bends to his task.
The pencil pausing and swooping like
a magnanimous sea bird that leaves a fish behind
instead of taking one as he draws
first from model, then memory
(the cat deserting the dish to explore
a scrabbling in the baseboards). Urgency
and calm balanced this one moment in his hand,
but no haste, no panic, the Panic of 1893

not here yet, however foreshadowed
by the bicycle-tire meat and drooping greens
he pushed aside tonight to get to work.
And so, it is

irrelevant that he's again tomorrow a farrier
or a marzipan maker or a shoe salesman;
who for now is nothing, a glass emptied
of the straining after profit in this world
to make room for this. If not tonight, then
the next, or another that, having drawn
the last inverted satin V of an ear, or
corrected the cant in the dish's base,
he'll set name and date at the bottom
before blotting out the light. And then
perhaps will forget it entirely, confusing it
with days of sawing joists, or counting licorice,
or oiling hackney seats

as it's passed along from closet shelf to
empty cigar box to pages of a neglected book.
To hang here now, what survives of
a moment of celebration from a half-lit life
while this night someone like he, and also different,
writes this.

## Analogous

Churchill called it his "black dog." As did,
we read, both Johnson and Boswell
(which, to score it fairly, counts for the same voice).
For another, it was Sleeping Beauty (see:
the thorns asphyxiating the castle walls and
the deadening sleep, non-inclusive of a timely
prince with jumper-cable kisses).

To which I add my own, to name the strangeness
that interposes between us, keeping its own hours.

It's an elevator shaft for one, vulture of the heart,
garden where you go anvil-picking.

It's your learner's permit grave, cave with no clearance
for the rest of us, the ledge you fall from
when we, walking beside you, have no inkling of the skyscraper.

Quicksand in the parade's path. Houdini mystifying
by stepping into chains. The wilderness where
you lie with a thousand snakebites, while I hold the map
upside-down by the fire, each stray boulder looking like the next.

# The Fealty of Neurons

You must forget everything that has happened.
After which you must strain water from a brick,
climb a mountain by a butter rope, mine iridium
from an old boot found in the cattails by the dam.

You must fold fire origami, drink feldspar
through a straw, breed an elephant from
two milkweed seeds and a garden hose. After
your well has gone dry in the fearsome drought.

You need to spit-polish lightning, drive a stake through
a cardinal's song, move rice grains with tweezers in a cyclone.
You need to find a cause that offends no one,
to make a war that brings children gorgeous dreams.

You must place your mind in sawdust piles on the floor.
After which you can begin to forget what happened
in the room that you cannot leave, where the other's eyes
are abducting you even as you walk among us.

# Tableau in the New Year

A yard overtaken by snow.
No sign anyone has tracked
the thirty-odd feet to the back fence
to free the midget spruce being
strangled leisurely. The landscape
may have once admitted to a sandbox here,
a garden path, but now returns
a blank stare. For the armchair
dreamers, the desert island's
conveniently brought to *them*.
This yard the same as the next, the same
as an hour ago, the same as tomorrow.
In a patio chair, a scarecrow block
of snow, not quite shapeless enough to
rule out a purposeful hand.
The house is cold and dark, like a thumb
clobbered yesterday with a hammer.
Whoever lives here sleeps a little longer
each night, will be slower
to notice when the ice cracks
this March in the watering can.

# Endgame

*For my father*

The king—which protests being thought of
as such—takes an arthritic sidestep
to the next column. As good as
if he'd vanished behind a panel
in the castle throne room. In pursuit,
a worldly bishop, three pawns, the sidesaddle knight,
and a somewhat blockheaded rook. Danged
if they know how to deal with him.
The king shrewdly denies everything:
the square-at-a-time circumscription,
the attrition of pieces on his end of the board.
The fact, in fact, of a game.
The knight moves awkwardly from one hitching post
to the next, arriving always to find the tavern
just deserted. The bishop has lost
the ability to think a move ahead.
Only the king understands how necessary it is
on each side—when evening wrings light
from a spent November sky—
for loss to feel like draw.

## D for Deuterium

To stalemate its use,
twenty-seven seven-liter flasks
of heavy water, smuggled from occupied Norway
at the *public* airport while the Nazis
kept their eyes on the wrong target
in a game of two-plane monte (great stuff!).
Thence to the vaults of the Curies' son-
in-law in Paris, after which
for better security the death cell
of a suburban prison (the SS not dreaming
that combat could harbor literalists).
They moved it across the Channel
in a collier, though not before getting the crew
drunk on champagne to buy time
for loading the holds. In Britain,
another prison briefly until at last,
after being swashbuckled this far,
it passed to the custody of
the royal librarian at Windsor Castle.
Who, between cataloging a minuet
of Henry VIII and restitching Macaulay's papers,
no doubt did his duty.

# The Children's Crusade

The epidemic took many, weakened more.
Parents stowed a shovel behind the pram in the closet,
used the back of the "it's a girl/boy" sign
to scribble out "quarantine." Summer nights in the cities
quieted to the sound of flies lighting on sills,
the balloon man releasing his unsold stock into the wild.

Naturally, they looked for causes to the macro world.
All things they'd invented or dealt, by turn,
became suspect, must be the cause: *viz.*, street dust,
resold bedding, cornflakes, subway cars, escaped
gases from grenade factories, white clothing,
ice-cream cones, excavations, aluminum leaching
from spatulas and forks, and metal money
(only when tucked impishly into the mouth).

They never dreamed a virus
could pull its tiny circus wagons from one to the next
and mesmerize. Or that it would be defeated soon
by white-coated women and men, many of whom
occupied these same cradles for now. Intolerable,
the notion that these ill ones inhabited a vast prairie of time
and missed by a blade of grass, the width
of an aphid's eye, being borne up whole.

## Third Strike

Doing a nickel in medium security
(who'd guess that a thrift shop would invest
in a *second* alarm?), and within hailing distance
of his parole. Preferred the splendid isolation
of his cell (snug, determinate), but cajoled once
into a softball game against the braggarts of D Block.
And, during the less-than-two percent of his outdoor time
that week, was drifting back on a fly ball when
the lightning bolt came down like heaven's shrimp fork
and found him. Was returned to an even closer space,
spare and beveled, for his bald escape out the front gates
(the sister from Fond du Lac weeping genuine tears).
And the ball lay outside the fences for months,
like a cabbage lacking the purpose of a salad bowl,
penitent and unslawed.

# Stealing Hymnals from the Choir

These are the famished in spirit.
They steal tomatoes from where the armless man
made his garden, sharpen their knives
on the gravestones of martyrs.

Be slow to invite them to your table.
They will scrape salt into their pockets,
hide the soup tureens in their laps,
use tweezers to serve your grandfather his salad.

They steal hymnals from the choir,
blood from blood banks. Last week at midnight,
one dug a sapling from the schoolyard,
where now the children vanish as they run.

These are the famished in spirit.
They sweep the world of its joy, using your broom
and mine. You will not know them by their fruits,
for they will have eaten them out of rancor and fear.

# Clover

Green tautologies, fairways, earth-hugging lawns,
anything that's held a beat too long, over, over,
over, where the intent's to starve out doubt,
prevent the ground-up parachuting of clover,

breeds a deeper doubt. As if the things
we architect or prune should have no ver-
tical push we don't dispense. We make hybrid orthodoxies,
co-opt signs of difference, lay highways where clover-

leaf is a sign of order. And so discourage right turns,
endings that just miss, how small praises of clover
can morph to the desirability of rough-edged longings—
a hint of falseness in the touch of a lover.

## Abundance

If you have only one finger, quoth the piano player,
you have something to say. One eye, and
you can find a galaxy where others sneezed and missed.
One ear, and you can hear the volcano while
the town dances noisy mambos . . . and save
the children. In a universe so tall, five grains of sand
and one hundred fit the same definition of plenty.

If you have only one idea, you will prosper in place
until earth pulls you under from sheer weight.
One belief, and you will enjoy your god
at amusement-park-ride heights until the day is done.
If you have one way to love, your heart
will make its crossing like pepper in the cargo hold,
while seabirds grab fish and punctuate the sky.

# Acknowledgments

"Ghost Town Fire" appeared in *White Pelican Review.*

"The Man Who Fell Asleep Inside a Moose" and "The Ex-Lover Speaks" appeared in *The Comstock Review.*

"Jellyfish in the Vineyard" and "The Accompanist" appeared in *Slant.*

"Shipwreck Survivors March Along the Coastline" and "Two-Timing the Beekeeper" appeared in *The Bryant Literary Review.*

"The Untruth" appeared in *The Alembic.*

"Will" appeared in *Perigee.*

"First Causes" and "The Fealty of Neurons" appeared in *Broken Bridge Review.*

"Black Widower" and "Trustee" appeared in *Coe Review.*

"The Church of His Debit-Card Soul" appeared in *The Externalist.*

"Geneticists in the Siege" appeared in *California Quarterly.*

"Exchange" appeared in *FutureCycle Poetry.*

"And We Blame You for Our Bad Dancing Too" appeared in *Oracle.*

"Salvage Alongside the Enemy" and "For Those Who Love" appeared in *Sangam.*

"Clams" appeared in *Common Ground Review.*

"The King's Cellars," "Inventory," "Four-Way Stop," and "Analogous" appeared at *The Write Room.*

"Eighth Rest" and "Pet Store Expecting Fish Gets Man's Body" appeared in *Freshwater.*

*Book design: Cover art by Ivan Hafizov (ivanhafizov.ru); photo of the author by Lon Horwedel (lonhorwedel@annarbor.com); design and typography by Diane Kistner (dkistner@futurecycle.org); body type, Candara with Poor Richard titling.*

# The FutureCycle Poetry Book Prize

FutureCycle Press conducts an annual full-length poetry book competition open to any poet writing in the English language. The winning manuscript is normally published over the summer, with the poet receiving a $1,000 prize plus 25 copies of the published book. Finalists may also be offered publishing contracts. Submissions of book manuscripts are accepted from January 1 to March 31 each year for that year's prize. The press also publishes individual poems in its online magazine, *FutureCycle Poetry*. These poems, which remain online indefinitely, are collected into an annual print edition each November.

To be considered, all submissions must be received via our online submission form. To avoid unnecessary delays or unread returns of submitted work, poets should review our guidelines:

*www.futurecycle.org/guidelines.aspx*

# Poetry Books
## from FutureCycle Press

### FutureCycle Poetry Book Prize Winners

*Stealing Hymnals from the Choir* by Timothy Martin (2010)
*No Loneliness* by Temple Cone (2009)

### FutureCycle Poetry Book Prize Finalists

*Castaway* by Katherine Riegel (2010 Finalist)
*Simple Weight* by Tania Runyan (2010 Finalist)
*Luminous Dream* by Wally Swist (2010 Finalist)
*Beyond the Bones* by Neil Carpathios (2009 Finalist)

### Full-length Books

*The Porous Desert* by David Chorlton
*Violet Transparent* by Anne Coray

### Chapbooks

*Colma* by John Laue
*Scything* by Joanne Lowery
*A Love Letter to Say There Is No Love* by Maria Russell-Williams